The
NORTH YORKSHIRE
MOORS RAILWAY
Past and Present
Volume 5

NORTH YORKSHIRE MOORS RAILWAY

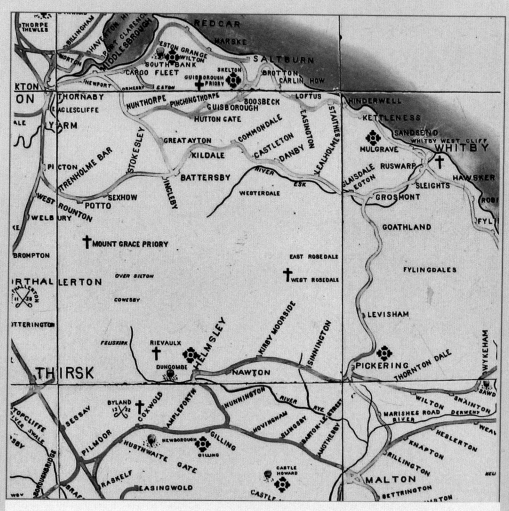

This extract from the iconic NER tiled map shows how the lines from Whitby to Malton, Middlesbrough and Picton related to the NER network.

A *PAST and PRESENT* Companion

The
NORTH YORKSHIRE
MOORS RAILWAY
Past and Present
Volume 5

John Hunt

Past & Present Books

First published in 2020

British Library Cataloguing in Publication Data

A catalogue record for this book is available from the British Library.

ISBN 978 1 85895 301 4
ISBN 978 1 85895 302 1

Past & Present Books
Mortons Media Group Limited
Media Centre
Morton Way
Horncastle
LN9 6JR
Tel/Fax: 01507 529535

email: sohara@mortons.co.uk
Website: www.nostalgiacollection.com

Acknowledgements

In compiling this book the author is indebted to the following: J. W. Armstrong, Simon Barraclough, Philip Benham, Dave Birtle, P. B. Booth, John Boyes, Maurice Burns, Nick Carter, Frank Dean, Chris Gammell, David Idle, Paul Jameson, R. H. King, Roy Lambeth, David Mitchell, NYMR collection, R. F. Payne, Geoff Plumb, Peter J. Robinson, Dave Rodgers, Ken Snowdon, John Spencer Gilks, David Sutcliffe, Luke Taylor, Nigel Trotter, Peter Walton, David Warren, E. R. Wethersett and John Whiteley.

For the Limited Edition I am also indebted to Bryan Blundell, Mike Braham, Murray Brown, Ian Broadhead, Peter Carleton, Craig Donald, Colin Graham, Heritage Railway Association, Ed Holman, Andrew Jeffery, John Midcalf, Terry Newman, D. Pollard, Peter W. Robinson, Richard Simpson and Roger Swift.

Contents

Half title page: 'J27' No 65894 passes Abbott's House, south of Goathland, with LNER teak coaches on 25 October 2018. *John Hunt*

This is the fifth volume dedicated to the NYMR, the third in colour, and, like the previous volume, not only covers the line from Whitby to Pickering and on to Malton, but also the Esk Valley line from Grosmont to Battersby and Middlesbrough.

The line from Whitby to Malton was originally the Whitby & Pickering Railway of 26 May 1836. The line was connected to the rapidly developing national network when it was extended southwards to join the York-Scarborough line at Rillington Junction, opening on 1 July 1845. It had connections at Bog Hall, Whitby, with the lines to Loftus (opened 3 December 1883, closed 5 May 1958) and Scarborough (opened 16 July 1885, closed 8 March 1965); at Grosmont with the Esk Valley line to Middlesbrough (opened 2 October 1865); and at Mill Lane, Pickering, with the Forge Valley line to Seamer (opened 1 April 1882, closed 3 January 1950) and the line to Helmsley and Pilmoor (opened 1 April 1875, closed 31 January 1953). In the meantime, the original rope-worked incline at Beckhole had proved a major stumbling block, so a 3½-mile Deviation line was built between Grosmont and Goathland, opening on 1 July 1865. The section of the original route between Grosmont and Beckhole, then Esk Valley, was retained for goods traffic until that also closed, on 18 September 1951.

The line flourished, with through coaches between London King's Cross and Whitby, as well as excursion traffic; there were even camping coaches for holidaymakers at Levisham, Goathland and Grosmont stations. However, following the war the rise in car ownership and burgeoning bus services meant a gradual decline in passenger traffic, which ultimately led to closure as a consequence of Dr Beeching's report, *The Re-shaping of British Railways*, published in March 1963, with its recommendations of closure of all the routes to Whitby. On 8 March 1965 the lines from Whitby to Scarborough and from Grosmont to Rillington Junction were duly closed, with only the Whitby-Middlesbrough line reprieved. The section of line from New Bridge to Rillington Junction remained open for freight until it, too, succumbed on 1 July 1966.

The loss of the local lines led to widespread concerns, especially in the Goathland area, and thoughts turned to the possibility of reopening under private ownership. Matters came to a head when rumours abounded that track-lifting was imminent, which led to a meeting at Tom Salmon's house at Ruswarp on 3 June 1967, which was a precursor to the setting up of the North Yorkshire Moors Railway Preservation Society (NYMRPS) at its inaugural meeting at Goathland on 18 November that year. Its aim was to reopen the 18-mile line from Grosmont to Pickering, both as a tourist railway and to preserve the rail link to Goathland, which was prone to being cut off by snow in winter.

The rest, as they say, is history! The Society quickly went from strength to strength. The first rolling stock – AC Cars railbus No W79978 – arrived on 9 August 1968, followed by the first steam engine – *Mirvale* – on 2 February 1969, traversing the whole line from Pickering to Grosmont in the process! In late 1968 volunteers were allowed access to the line, and over the next few years more locomotives and rolling stock arrived, and the track and stations were brought back into operation.

A major step forward came on 1 May 1973, when the line was officially reopened, and on 24 May 1975 steam trains once more travelled regularly between Grosmont and Pickering. The next 30 years saw consolidation, with gradual and incremental improvements to rolling stock and infrastructure, and ever-increasing patronage, helped by worldwide exposure in TV series like *Heartbeat* and the first 'Harry Potter' film.

In 2007 another major milestone was the extension of NYMR services over Network Rail tracks to and from Whitby. In 2014 the clock was turned back when a second platform was reinstated at Whitby station. When the NYMR celebrated its 50th anniversary in 2017 it was able to reflect that it had come a long way since 1967; it now carried around 320,000 passengers each year, had an annual turnover of more than £5,000,000, employed more than 100 paid staff in the peak season, and was supported by an even greater number of volunteers, who actually ran the trains, a far cry from the low point in its fortunes back in March 1965. A more comprehensive history of the railway and further details about its services can be obtained from the NYMR website, www.nymr.co.uk.

While the economic and hardship case for closure of the lines from Whitby to Scarborough and Rillington was upheld, the reprieve for the line from Middlesbrough to Whitby was primarily based on the need to provide transport for schoolchildren from the villages in the Esk Valley to the secondary school in Whitby, a role it still performs today. However, the reprieve did not come without cost savings, and since 1965 the line from Nunthorpe has seen major rationalisation, with Whitby reduced from four platforms to just one, station staff withdrawn, the track singled between Whitby and Grosmont, the crossing loop at Castleton removed, and signalling and signal boxes replaced with the 'No Signaller Token System on Single Lines with Remote Crossing Loops' (NSTR), controlled from Nunthorpe signal box.

The 17¼-mile line from Grosmont to Battersby consists of the Grosmont & Castleton branch, opened by the NER on 2 October 1865, which met the North Yorkshire & Cleveland Railway (NY&CR) at Castleton, thus providing a through route between Whitby and the Leeds Northern main line at Picton (the Battersby-Picton section closed on 14 June 1954, though the section from Battersby to Stokesley lingered on until 2 August 1965). The final section of the NY&CR had opened to Castleton in 1861, two years after the North Eastern Railway (NER) had taken it over.

The 11-mile line from Battersby to Middlesbrough was instigated partly by the North Yorkshire & Cleveland Railway, with the 5½ miles to Nunthorpe East Junction (for Guisborough, closed on 2 March 1964), and partly by the Middlesbrough & Guisborough Railway, which was opened to passengers in 1854. Between Nunthorpe East Junction and Middlesbrough, a distance of another 5½ miles, there were two

intermediate stations, at Nunthorpe itself and at Ormesby, but on 3 May 1976 a new halt was opened at Gypsy Lane, just three-quarters of a mile north of Nunthorpe. Ormesby was later renamed Marton, and on 18 May 2014 another new station was opened to serve the massive James Cook University Hospital complex, situated between Marton and Middlesbrough. North of Nunthorpe, in 2017 the Whitby service of four trains a day was augmented by local services to and from Newcastle, such that up to 17 trains traversed this section of line each way, every weekday.

The fortunes of the 35-mile Whitby-Middlesbrough line have been turned round, since it is now supported by the Esk Valley Railway Development Company (EVRDC) set up in 2003, which was designated by the Department for Transport as a Community Rail Partnership in 2005. Apart from the essential service of bringing Esk Valley students to school, the number of visitors to Whitby has grown since 2003. The EVRDC promotes and markets the line, distributes timetables throughout the Esk Valley and highlights the need for an improved service. Further EVRDC details are obtainable from: enquiries@eskvalleyrailway.co.uk.

On 26 April 2019 the late Ken Snowdon walked deep into the heart of Newtondale and got this superb picture of No 80136 on the 11.00 train from Pickering.

This general view of Whitby station was taken from the tall signal box in August 1964.

No 156438 awaits departure from Whitby as the 16.00 service to Middlesbrough on 14 May 2020. The photographer has tried to emulate Frank Dean's 1964 vantage point from the old station signal box, now long since demolished and, together with the platforms and goods shed on the right, now replaced by a Co-op store. Note that in this and the next 'present' picture, the buildings on the left and on the skyline are little changed. *Frank Dean/Luke Taylor (with apologies to Dave Birtle)*

A different perspective of Whitby station shows a DMU departing with the 11.22 service to Scarborough on 3 March 1965.

No 156438 is seen again departing from Whitby as the 16.00 service to Middlesbrough on 14 May 2020. In 2014 it was possible to rebuild a second platform at Whitby, together with an engine release road, which had the combined effect of allowing an increase in the number of through trains from Pickering to five a day, greatly simplifying the process of locomotives running round their trains, and, crucially, giving a great boost to passenger numbers travelling over the NYMR to and from Whitby. *Frank Dean/Luke Taylor (with apologies to Dave Birtle)*

No 61319 stands in Platform 2 at Whitby with a train from Malton in August 1964.
　　Another 'B1', this time No 61264, stands in the same place having arrived on a charter from York on 18 March 2017. *Frank Dean/John Hunt*

Viewed from Windsor Terrace, No 142018 awaits departure with a service for Middlesbrough.
No 156490 is about to depart with the midday train to Middlesbrough on 23 January 2017. *Both John Hunt*

With the abbey dominating the skyline, a DMU arrives at Platform 1 at Whitby some time in 1962.
In a similar view from gardens in Windsor Terrace, No 45407 arrives at Whitby on 3 April 2017.
David Sutcliffe/John Hunt

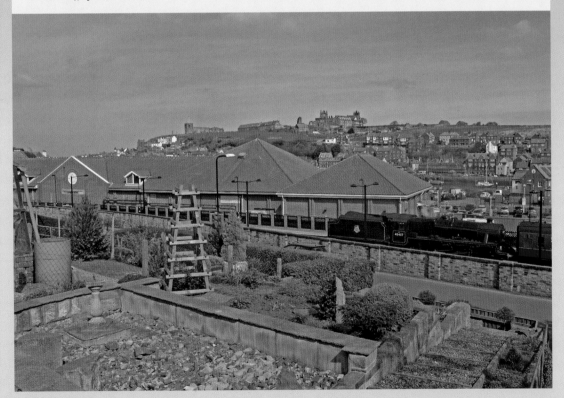

No 2005 awaits departure from Whitby with a special to Battersby on 28 June 1975. Above the tender is the building recovered in 1990 and re-erected at Pickering in 1992/93.
    No 156490 leaves Whitby forming the 11.58 service to Middlesbrough on 23 January 2017.
Chris Gammell/John Hunt

A DMU arrives at Whitby on 8 March 1965. While the engine shed on the left is long since disused, the goods yard on the right is still very much in business.

No 62005 departs from the new platform at Whitby against the backdrop of the abbey with a train to Pickering on 6 April 2016. Although the engine shed remains, the goods sheds and goods yard have long gone, now replaced by a Coop store and a large car park. *Frank Dean/John Hunt*

No 61018 *Gnu* shunts the goods yard on 14 May 1964. The photographer had travelled in the brake van from Malton, taking pictures en route.

Another 'B1', No 1264, shunts round its train at Whitby on 9 October 2019. New houses have appeared in front of the old engine shed and the goods yard is now a massive car park, but the buildings beyond the railway to the left, centre and right are readily recognisable. *John Boyes/John Hunt*

D6780 shunts the Whitby-Tees Yard pick-up goods at Whitby on 3 March 1965.

No 62005 leaves Whitby with the 12.45 train to Pickering on 3 October 2019. The tracks serving the goods yard on the right are long gone and new houses occupy the area of the former locomotive yard on the left, the trees obscuring the houses beyond. However, the white-gabled building on the extreme right is common to both pictures. *Frank Dean/John Hunt*

1975 saw limited steam operation on the Esk Valley line between Grosmont, Whitby and Battersby, as part of the Stockton & Darlington 150 celebrations, and in subsequent years there were occasional forays onto the line to Whitby. However, the NYMR harboured visions of restoring regular through services from Pickering to Whitby by running its own trains over the 6 miles of Network Rail line between Grosmont and the town, and in 2007 the vision became reality when the railway secured its own safety case and passenger licence to meet Network Rail requirements. Thirty-two years before, with the abbey and the River Esk as a backdrop, No 2005 leaves Whitby for Battersby on 8 June 1975.

From a similar viewpoint standing on the formation of the spur line from Bog Hall to Prospect Hill, No 45407 is seen leaving Whitby with a train for Pickering on 3 April 2017. The bridge in the background carries the town centre avoiding road and was officially opened by the Marquis of Normandy in 1980. *Both John Hunt*

A DMU climbs up to Prospect Hill Junction from Bog Hall Junction with the 12.50 Middlesbrough-Scarborough service on 26 February 1965. After reversal at Prospect Hill, the DMU will continue its journey across Larpool Viaduct over the River Esk in the background.

This is a similar vantage point on 20 March 2017. Although the trackbed is a footpath, tree growth has made an exact comparison impossible. *John Spencer Gilks/John Hunt*

Prospect Hill Junction signal box is seen in 1965 looking north from the line coming up from Bog Hall. The bridge beyond carries the Whitby-Middlesbrough road, and through it can just be glimpsed Whitby West Cliff station, by now no longer served by trains.

The present-day view was taken on 20 March 2017. The footpath is part of the Cinder Track walk along the old railway from Whitby to Scarborough. *Frank Dean/John Hunt*

This is another view of the 12.50 Middlesbrough-Scarborough DMU having reversed direction in the top left of the picture and now resuming its journey to Scarborough by crossing over the Bog Hall line and the River Esk via the imposing Larpool Viaduct.

In the present-day view, taken on 20 March 2017, tree growth has all but hidden the old trackbeds, though part of the retaining wall is still visible. *John Spencer Gilks/John Hunt*

Viewed from the lofty height of Larpool Viaduct, by now a public footpath, the gas works was still active, with its rail connection extant, on 8 June 1975, as No 2005 worked into Whitby with a return charter train from Battersby.

From the same vantage point, No 45407 approaches Larpool on 3 April 2017. Although the gas holders have long gone, two of the red-brick buildings survive. *Both John Hunt*

A DMU heads out of Whitby towards Ruswarp some time in 1964. On the right is the line from Bog Hall to Prospect Hill, which at one time connected Whitby's Town and West Cliff stations.

In the 'going away' view of No 45407 on 3 April 2017, the trackbed of the spur line from Bog Hall to Prospect Hill is marked by the two electricity poles. *David Mitchell/John Hunt*

In the first picture No 2005 accelerates out of Whitby and under Larpool Viaduct with a special train to Battersby on 8 June 1975.

Pictured in the same place, unit No 144021 forms a service to Middlesbrough on 16 April 2002. In the intervening years the Captain Cook residential development has changed the view.

Finally, No 62005 heads under Larpool Viaduct with a Whitby to Pickering train on 23 April 2016. *All John Hunt*

No 2005 rounds the curve from Larpool Viaduct, paralleling the River Esk at low tide, with a returning excursion from Whitby to London St Pancras, 'The Eskdale Venturer', on 28 June 1975. The 'K1' took the train as far as Battersby, where Class 45 diesel No 45121 took over again for the run back to London.

No 144021 has just passed under Larpool Viaduct with a service to Middlesbrough on 19 November 2003. By this time the old down line had been removed and riverside vegetation had grown appreciably. *Both John Hunt*

A DMU heads away from Whitby in August 1964, alongside the River Esk towards Ruswarp, visible in the distance.
   The corresponding view was taken on 15 February 2019, and dominating both views is St Bartholomew's Church. *Frank Dean/John Hunt*

These views of Ruswarp station were taken on 9 August 1966 and 13 April 2014. *Frank Dean/John Hunt*

Ruswarp station is first seen from the footpath over the River Esk in 1963.

Next, No 156471 leaves Ruswarp with a Whitby-Middlesbrough service in November 2007; the gates, signals and signal box have gone, replaced by automatic barriers and flashing lights.

The same view on 11 October 2019 shows No 62005 on the 12.30 Whitby-Goathland train; the bridge deck has been replaced and the footway on the right, from which the first two pictures were taken, removed altogether. *David Sutcliffe/John Hunt (2)*

No 61276 crosses the River Esk at Ruswarp with a train from York to Whitby in 1964.
'B1' No 1264 crosses the River Esk with the 14.00 Whitby-Pickering train on 9 October 2019. The top of the road bridge can just be glimpsed above the first coach. *John Boyes/John Hunt*

These are Chain Bridge Cottages, west of Ruswarp, looking west in the summer of 1966, and on 4 April 2017. *Frank Dean/John Hunt*

No 31128 enters Sleights station with the return pick-up goods from Whitby to Tees Yard.
From the same vantage point, unit No 156482 arrives at the station on 4 April 2017.
John Spencer Gilks/John Hunt

Looking west at Sleights, the pick-up goods returns to Tees Yard on 30 August 1968.

No 156482 leaves Sleights for Middlesbrough on 4 April 2017. The building on the disused down platform was relocated to Grosmont by the NYMR in 1989. *Frank Dean/John Hunt*

The last Malton-Whitby train leaves Sleights on 6 March 1965. While the passenger service from Grosmont to Malton was to be withdrawn from the same day, the line to Middlesbrough was to remain open. There appears to be healthy coal traffic in the adjacent goods yard.

No 156463 leaves Sleights forming the 11.58 Whitby-Newcastle service on 25 February 2020. Only the old up platform is in use today, though the other is still in situ, as is the small signal box at the Whitby end of the station, visible in the 'past' picture, but now obscured by tree growth. The old coal yard, which soldiered on after the cessation of the pick-up freight, has returned to nature. However, the large tree on the left, the station house above the train and the house on the right are instantly recognisable in the two pictures. *Frank Dean/John Hunt*

No 61049 approaches Sleights with the York-Whitby pick-up goods on 25 May 1964.

From a similar viewpoint No 61264 slows for the Sleights stop with a charter train from York on 18 March 2017. *John Boyes/John Hunt*

Grosmont

Major improvements by the NYMR to the track layout at the north end of Grosmont station are seen in June 1989. The double slip was installed to allow the Esk Valley line, on the right, access to and from platforms 2 and 3, and to serve two carriage sidings off to the bottom left.

An identical viewpoint is no longer possible following the removal, in 2002, of the brickworks bridge that spanned the track here, after it was damaged by a rail-mounted crane carrying out work on the Esk Valley line. However, this is the best alternative view on 22 February 2019. The signal gantry came from Falsgrave at Scarborough and, foreshortened, was recommissioned in 2014. *Both John Hunt*

The previous 'past' picture was taken from the brickworks bridge in the background, which connected the brickworks with the iron works. Nos 30926 *Repton* and 3672 *Dame Vera Lynn* await their next turns of duty in the spring of 2000.

In the corresponding view No 62005 brings a train from Whitby into the station on 19 April 2019, while No D7628 awaits its next Whitby turn. The bridge buttresses both remain but are not visible in this view. *Both John Hunt*

No 37059 brings the Whitby-Tees Yard pick-up goods into Grosmont station on a September day in 1981.

No 156487 is seen at the same spot as it departs from Grosmont with the 10.35 Middlesbrough-Whitby service on 17 October 2019. Much has changed in the intervening period – both platforms have been extended, the Esk Valley line has been slewed to the left, and the junction with the NYMR is now beyond the signal gantry. *Both John Hunt*

A DMU diverges from the Malton line at Grosmont forming a Whitby-Middlesbrough service in the summer of 1964.

The same view on 3 April 2019 shows Met-Cam DMU No 101685 waiting to depart for Pickering. Platforms 3 and 4 have been extended – note the change from stonework to red brick marking the northern end of the original platform. The signal box was closed in 1972 and dismantled in 1979, although the upper part was reused in the signal box at Alston on the South Tynedale Railway. *Frank Dean/John Hunt*

Grosmont station house and level crossing are pictured in July 1964 and on 18 April 2017.
Frank Dean/John Hunt

No D7029 impatiently idles away, waiting for the Grosmont postmistress to remove her washing on 4 September 1985.

In a similar view from 3 April 2019 visiting No 34092 *City of Wells* prepares to leave with the dining train in what is now platform 4. The original up platform has been extended to make an island platform, but the old waiting shelter remains, now used as a catering store. The building on the right was built in 1835 by the W&PR as a goods warehouse; the large double doors originally allowed goods vehicles to enter via a 10-foot wagon turntable. *David Idle/John Hunt*

On a warm summer's day, No 1247 departs from Grosmont on 4 August 1975.

By contrast, the snow lies thick on the ground as No 6619 departs on 28 December 1985.

Chris Gammell/John Hunt

In the first picture a DMU awaits the 'right away' forming a Whitby-York service in July 1964.

Next we see *Salmon* (left) and No 3 shunting at Grosmont in April 1969.

Finally, another DMU is seen awaiting departure, for Pickering, on 9 March 2018. The new signal box, of a hybrid construction, dates from 1994. *Frank Dean/ John Boyes/John Hunt*

No 63395 is ready for departure from Grosmont station for Goathland on 27 June 1970. Note the gate box on the left, against the Grosmont Coop wall, which was the NYMR's first working signal box.

The same vantage point offers a much changed scene, as No 62005 departs from Grosmont with the 10.00 Whitby-Pickering train on 3 October 2019. *Both John Hunt*

This was the view south from the level crossing at Grosmont in August 1968. On the right is the gate cabin, demolished in 1996, and through the tunnel can be glimpsed Deviation signal box.

From the same viewpoint on 22 February 2019 the cabin and signal have gone and the gates replaced. *John Boyes/John Hunt*

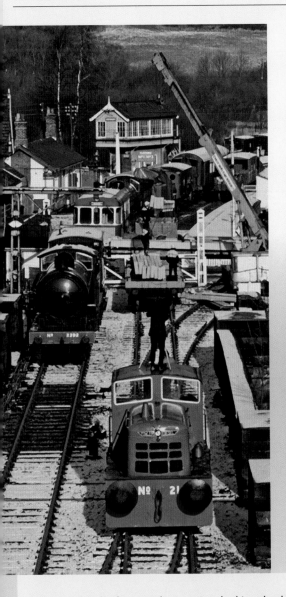

Steelwork for the first new locomotive shed is unloaded onto rail wagons at Grosmont level crossing for hauling through the tunnel to the shed site by No 21 in February 1975.

Pictured from the top of Grosmont Tunnel, in the same view, No 65894 leaves Grosmont on 30 March 2019. *Both John Hunt*

Tunnel Cottages, still in use at the time for volunteer accommodation, are seen on the left, the NER ballast brake in the middle, and Deviation signal box in the distance, pictured from the tunnel mouth in the autumn of 1971.

There's a rather different scene from the same viewpoint on 18 April 2017. *Nick Carter/John Hunt*

This view of the new loco shed in May 1974 was taken while Tunnel Cottages were still in use. In front of them are the Gloucester C&W DMU, 'Q6' No 3395 and the GNR coach.

In the second view No 2392 is lifted by two road cranes after running a hot axlebox in July 1975 immediately prior to the locomotive's appearance at the S&D 150 celebrations at Shildon.

From the same view on 18 April 2017, the original shed can just be glimpsed to the left, but in front of it is the fabrication shop, hiding the two-road running shed behind it (1990), the wheeldrop shed to the right (2011), coaling plant (1989), and the Armstrong Oilers building, opened in 2005, in the foreground.
All John Hunt

Stages in the building of the first loco shed: in the first view, dated May 1971, the first inspection pit has been dug and concreted by the Territorial Army; left to right, John Hardy, Nigel Trotter, Don Robertson and Jeff Brand are about to cover the newly laid concrete to protect it from possible frost damage.

In the second view diesel shunter No 21 brings another wagon load of steel framing to the site in February 1973. Track has been laid over the pit and into the shed site, where the sheer legs from Tweedmouth have already been erected.

Next, by March 1973 erection of the steel-framed building was well advanced.

Two years later, in March 1975, the frame was complete and roofed over and the brick walls are in an advanced stage of construction. Also, a second track has been laid into the shed.

Finally, from a similar viewpoint on 18 April 2017, a 'Weltrol' wagon carrying a 'Black Five' boiler is standing on the short pit, and to its right is part of the fabrication shop constructed in 1996.
All John Hunt

Sheer legs, capable of hydraulically lifting the end of a locomotive or tender, were primarily used to remove wheelsets if axleboxes required attention, and were based at most of the larger LNER motive power depots. This set was rescued by the NELPG from the depot at Tweedmouth, on the south side of the River Tweed at Berwick, and dismantled by volunteers, loaded onto rail wagons and delivered to Grosmont from Tees Yard on the Whitby pick-up goods.

In the first picture they have been re-erected at Grosmont early in 1973 in advance of the construction of the shed around them, while in the second view they are doing the job they were designed for, in this instance removing the trailing truck and rear driving wheel from No 29 in October 1977. *Both John Hunt*

The first steam-hauled train left Whitby on 4 June 1847 but had to change to rope haulage at Beckhole. In 1854 the Y&NMR became a founder member of the North Eastern Railway, and the new company regarded the steep rope-worked incline at Beckhole, between Grosmont and Goathland, to be a major hindrance. It therefore constructed a 4-mile diversionary line with easier gradients, which opened on 1 July 1865. The junction between the two lines was controlled by Deviation signal box, in the background of the first picture, showing a crane unloading the sheerlegs from Tweedmouth on 21 March 1970, which had arrived on wagons from the Whitby pick-up goods.

In the other corresponding views, almost the entire NYMR steam fleet is visible in the picture taken in June 1974, while in the last view, taken on 22 February 2019, the NELPG's Deviation shed occupies the site of the signal box, with the Armstrong Oilers building in the foreground. *Maurice Burns/John Hunt (2)*

The line was formally reopened by the Duchess of Kent on 1 May 1973 when she travelled by a Royal Train, headed by NER 'P3' 0-6-0 No 2392 and NCB 0-6-2T No 29, from Grosmont through to Pickering station. The special train is pictured working off Esk Valley Viaduct.

At the same spot, No 66016 heads a ballast train from Tees Yard bound for a NYMR track-relaying site on 3 February 2015. *Maurice Burns/John Hunt*

No 841 passes some splendid autumn colours at Beckhole with a Grosmont-Pickering train in the early 1980s.

No 45407 is pictured in the same location on 3 April 2017 with a Whitby-Pickering train – note the wholesale tree clearance on the right. *Both John Hunt*

No 220006 *Clyde Voyager* crosses the Eller Beck at Water Ark on 28 April 2002, while in the second picture visiting No 34081 *92 Squadron* crosses on 29 September 2018.
Both John Hunt

On 25 June 1970 the first BR steam locomotive – 'Q6' 0-8-0 No 63395 – arrived from Thornaby, via the Esk Valley line, together with former National Coal Board 0-6-2T No 29 from the extensive NCB system at Philadelphia, in County Durham. Here the 'Q6', working its first train in preservation, negotiates Water Ark two days later.

Some 45 years later, No 60007 *Sir Nigel Gresley* makes a superb sight at Water Ark on 27 April 2015. *Both John Hunt*

Borrows 0-4-0WT No 3 propels two H&BR wagons up the 1 in 49 gradient at Darnholm on a bitterly cold 7 December 1969. These two wagons now form innovate seating areas in the goods warehouse tea room on Goathland station.

A slightly larger and more modern locomotive, No 34092 *City of Wells*, is on the 15.40 Grosmont-Pickering train at the same spot on 4 April 2019. *John Boyes/John Hunt*

The first picture shows a 'B1' at Darnholm on a Whitby-Leeds train in 1964, and the second a three-car Metro-Cammell DMU, hired in from BR, leading the Gloucester C&W DMU at Darnholm in April 1973. Finally No 44806 climbs the last few yards to Goathland on 15 April 2017. *David Sutcliffe/ Nick Carter/John Hunt*

Goathland

A DMU travelling from Whitby to Malton arrives at Goathland on a snowy day in February 1964, then another Metro-Cammell DMU is pictured in the same place on 17 February 2015. *Frank Dean/John Hunt*

NORTH YORKSHIRE MOORS RAILWAY

In the first of these three photographs Goathland station is pictured in the summer of 1964, followed by a similar view in the winter of 1970, and the same scene on a pleasant 15 April 2017. *David Sutcliffe/ John Boyes/John Hunt*

A 'B1' enters the station with the 7.24pm to Malton on a lovely summer's evening in 1961.
    From a similar viewpoint, No 80136 arrives in Goathland station on 18 April 2017. The footbridge came from Howdon, on North Tyneside, following electrification of the Tyneside Metro, and was erected in 1985/86. *David Sutcliffe/John Hunt*

Some things don't change! Family holidaymakers await the arrival of their train home, first in July 1964 as No 61319 heads a Whitby-Malton train, then on 22 April 2017 with No 61264 entering Goathland station. *Frank Dean/ John Hunt*

The NYMRPS's first booking office at Goathland was erected in 1969, but was demolished in 1971 after the railway obtained access to the main station building. It was made from old fence rails, hardboard and a 'WD' 2-8-0 window frame, to a design by Dick Oxlade (the NYMR's 'Mr Fixit' at the time!).

The new, purpose-built shop on the same site is seen on 24 March 2017. *Nick Carter/ John Hunt*

A Metro-Cammell DMU forming the 10.25 York-Whitby service loads and unloads parcels and passengers at Goathland on 5 March 1965, just three days before closure.
  In similarly wintry weather Metro-Cammell DMU No 101685 makes its Goathland stop on 29 December 2017. *Frank Dean/John Hunt*

The railbus stands in the up platform at Goathland in March 1971.

The second view is also looking south from the down platform on 15 April 2017. A more modern coach to provide volunteer accommodation has replaced the Gresley sleeping car seen in the earlier picture, but nearest the camera is a camping coach for holiday hire, perpetuating a LNER and BR tradition here
R. H. King/John Hunt

During an early NYMPS gala at Goathland in June 1970, No 29 is arriving from Summit, then the extent of operations. On the left stands *Salmon* and, in steam, *Mirvale*, which would shunt the coaches to release No 29.

Looking south from the footbridge on 29 December 2017, the DMU awaits the arrival of No D7628 from Pickering. Since 1970 the BR bracket starting signal has been replaced by an LNER-pattern one on the far side of the water tower. *Both John Hunt*

From Easter 1970 it was possible for members to travel by steam train between Goathland and Summit. Here *Salmon* and *Mirvale* propel the well-patronised sleeping car out of Goathland on 26 April 1970 and across bridge No 27, the subject of a major fund-raising exercise in 2018/19 for its replacement.

The second view of bridge No 27 shows No 44806 on a Pickering-bound train on 2 April 2017.
John Boyes/John Hunt

One of the new beams of bridge No 27 crossing the Eller Beck at Goathland is craned into position with two NER steam cranes in 1908.

History in the making! The same bridge beam is successfully lifted out on 10 January 2020, seen from the same spot where the photographer stood in 1908 to record a very similar scene. The Volker Rail Kirov cranes are somewhat different (!) and H&S and PPE now bear no comparison, but the houses on the right are still there, as are the water tower and remnants of the Pelton Wheel and the stone crusher to its right. This was the first high-profile progress as a result of the success of the NYMR's Yorkshire's Magnificent Journey appeal and the resultant HLF grant. *NYMR Archive (originals in the NRM)/John Hunt*

Volunteers had been allowed access to the line from 10 December 1968, but in the meantime rolling stock for the fledgling scheme had started to arrive, being based in the up sidings at Goathland. Here the AC railbus is pictured on 30 June 1972.

In the very early days Goathland was the motive power depot, as shown in the second picture of Nos 5, 3395 and 3, in steam, on 30 August 1970. Note the volunteer accommodation on the extreme right – a tent!

Also viewed from the top of the water tower, No 3395 is ready to depart for Summit on a rather damp day in August 1971. *David Idle (2)/ John Hunt*

GNR No 1247 heads a three-coach train out of Goathland at Easter 1975, then on 15 February 2009 the DMU leaves the station for Pickering. *Both John Hunt*

On the occasion of the NELPG's fifth anniversary, its two locomotives, 'P3' 0-6-0 No 2392 and 'Q6' 0-8-0 No 3395, pass just south of Goathland on 2 November 1971.

No 45407 is captured in the same place with a Whitby-Pickering train on 3 April 2017. The coniferous trees have gone, and the signals have changed, but the rail-motor shed remains the same. *Chris Gammell/John Hunt*

Negotiations started with BR to retain a single track throughout, but while these proceeded contractors removed the second track between Grosmont and Levisham, and eventually all of the track south of Pickering. Working southwards, the track materials were taken out by train, with the final movement between Pickering and Rillington Junction taking place on 2 November 1969, and the line was severed south of Pickering on the same day. That summer, No D1517 stands at Burnett House bridge, Goathland, with a scrap recovery train.

D7628 is seen at the same place with a Pickering-bound train on 18 April 2017. *Roy Lambeth/John Hunt*

No 3395 makes brisk progress past Goathland's down distant signal with an empty stock train in the spring of 1971, while nearly half a century later No 66034 passes Abbots House with a trainload of ballast from Tees Yard to a track-relaying site in Newtondale on 1 March 2017. *Both John Hunt*

Moorgates is where a minor road to Goathland, from the main Pickering-Whitby road, crosses under the railway and, understandably, is a popular place to stop and watch the trains. In the first view, from June 1970, the AC Cars railbus heads back to Goathland from Summit.

An the same place in June 1992 No D7541 drops downhill to Goathland.

Finally, No 66078, at the head of a ballast train, passes Moorgates on 8 March 2017.
All John Hunt

In June 1970 No 29 returns from Goathland Summit and passes Moorgates, even then a popular place to watch the trains. Note the interesting selection of motor vehicles and the old cast-iron highway sign.

It's not quite as popular in this 3 April 2017 view as the DMU passes the same spot with a working from Pickering to Grosmont. *Both John Hunt*

In the early days, helping out with No 29 and the 'Q6', No 5 did its fair share of passenger operation between Goathland and Summit. Here, in the hands of driver Eric Blackburn, it passes Moorgates on 30 August 1970.

No 825 heads the NYMR's Pullman dining train at the same place on 28 October 2011.

John Hunt/Ken Snowdon

The Royal reopening train is seen again here, this time between Moorgates and Eller Beck on 1 May 1973. In almost the same place, 46 years later, No 65894 heads a Grosmont-Pickering train on 19 April 2019. *Maurice Burns/John Hunt*

With the famous Fylingdales 'golf balls' on the horizon and the Pickering-Whitby road full of holiday traffic, No 3395 stands at Goathland Summit on 31 August 1970.

The 'golf balls' have gone now, replaced by a pyramidal structure near Goathland Summit, as the DMU drops down towards Goathland on 4 April 2017. *David Idle/John Hunt*

Goathland Summit signal box is pictured first in the summer of 1967, then an August 1973 view slightly further south shows the points serving the summit relief siding, and volunteers recovering track materials. Part of the former double track had been retained and formed into a loop to allow locomotives to run round when Summit was the limit of operations.

The similar view on 22 February 2019 shows that, while the signal box has long gone, the wooden huts on either side of it just about survive. *Frank Dean/John Hunt (2)*

A gang of permanent way workers are pictured at Fen Bogs, then the second rare picture depicts Fen Bogs Houses. The OS map of 1954 shows them as ruins.

The same view in March 1974 shows No 5 passing the summit. Although now hidden by trees, the red-brick outhouse in the middle picture still stands, though in ruins.
NYMR collection (2)/ John Hunt

NYMR

NORTH YORKSHIRE
MOORS RAILWAY

'A6' 4-6-2T No 691 heads a Whitby-Malton train at Fen Bogs some time in the 1930s. Wagons stand in the NRCC siding in the distance, while at bottom right is the buffer stop of the summit relief siding. Evidence shows that the sidings were still in position in 1964 when the signal box diagram was redrawn. Also, John Mallon has a picture taken in 1962 showing the down sidings with bogie bolsters in them, and RAF Fylingdales under construction. Some rewiring was done to the Summit signal box in 1928 for the council sidings, which may indicate when they went in.

Also viewed from the fourth carriage, No 61264 crosses Fen Bogs on 15 April 2017.
E. R. Wethersett/John Hunt

A lone *Mirvale* nears the summit of the line on its epic journey from Pickering to Grosmont on 2 February 1969. In the second view two Gloucester DMUs pass the same place in July 1975, then No D7029 emerges from Northdale in June 1986. *All John Hunt*

A 'B1' heads south at Fen Bogs with a Saturdays-only Whitby to London King's Cross train in August 1964. Travelling in the opposite direction, No 45212 passes the same spot and approaches the Lyke Wake Walk crossing with a Pickering-Grosmont train on 30 April 2017. *Frank Dean/David Rodgers*

No 5 crosses Fen Bogs en route to Pickering in October 1977, then on 24 February 2019 DMU No 101685 is seen at the same location, passing one of only two remaining telegraph poles, complete with cross-pieces, still standing on the NYMR. *Both John Hunt*

No 5 is near bridge No 20 at the top of the climb through Northdale with a special train returning from Pickering in August 1971.

  At almost the same location, visiting No 46100 *Royal Scot* just about beats the encroaching shadows on 26 March 2017. *Both John Hunt*

Situated in Northdale, a continuation of Newtondale, not far short of the railway's MP 17, this former farmhouse, Nabs Head, was demolished to make way for a Forestry Commission track that ran from Levisham as far as Carters House.

The present-day view shows the site from the cab of No 80136 on a Goathland-bound train on 2 May 2019. Several BR Standard 2-6-4Ts were sent to Whitby when new in 1958. *NYMR collection/John Hunt*

The permanent way hut seen in the previous 'past' picture was replaced by a more modern hut, but this too was taken down in this summer 1969 view. While the old up line is still in situ, the down line is in the throes of being lifted. On the right stand a rail-motor and trailers, indispensable in the pioneering days of the infant NYMR.

At the same location No 63395 heads purposefully down grade with a goods train on 15 November 2007. The wooden telegraph pole on the right is common to both pictures! *Paul Jameson/John Hunt*

The 'past' view of Yew Tree Scar in the upper reaches of Newtondale was taken from a Malton to Whitby DMU in the winter of 1963. The same view on 30 December 2017 shows Newtondale Halt, now erected at this location. *David Sutcliffe/ John Hunt*

Though disused since the 1930s, Newtondale signal box still retained its nameboard in 1964, as seen in the first view. However, the nameboard and windows had gone by the summer of 1965. In the third picture, dated 14 February 2019, just the foundations are visible, although the telegraph pole is common to all three pictures. *David Sutcliffe/ Frank Dean/John Hunt*

The first steam locomotive to arrive on the embryonic NYMR was the diminutive Hudswell Clarke 0-4-0ST *Mirvale*, which was delivered by road to Pickering goods yard before steaming through to Grosmont on a snowy 2 February 1969. During a stop on the 1 in 49 gradient south of Newtondale signal box, NYMR pioneers Sid Midgeley (in the cab), Joe Brown and Tom Robertson engage in conversation on what was an historic occasion. The second picture shows the same location 50 years later, on 14 February 2019. *John Boyes/John Hunt*

This was the view looking north-east at MP14 in the summer of 1967, when the photographer walked the line through Newtondale with his wife, Heather.

Looking from the same vantage point on 11 March 2019, note the pole on the right and the remains of the fence on the left, common to both pictures. *Frank Dean/John Hunt*

Another result of Frank Dean's walk along the line from Levisham with his wife on 10 June 1967 is this picture of the catch point on the down line, just short of MP13, between Levisham station and The Grange. However, it appears to be secured in a rather ineffective position!

At the same spot on 11 March 2019, MP13 is still standing. *Frank Dean/John Hunt*

The BR weedkilling train leaves Levisham on its return from Pickering to Grosmont behind GNR No 1247 and 'Q6' No 63395 in July 1976.

On 16 February 2019 the DMU leaves Levisham for Grosmont. While the coniferous plantation has been felled, the deciduous trees have matured, all but obscuring the 'past' view. *Both John Hunt*

No 2005 performs a photographic runpast for NELPG members on 30 October 1986. Nowadays, exhausts such as this are very much frowned upon!

Twenty years later No 101685 enters Levisham as the 12.30 Grosmont-Pickering service on 17 October 2019. The down siding, on the left, was laid in 2005 as a training exercise by the British Army's 79th Railway Squadron. Note the 'limit of shunt' signal on the right, common to both pictures, and that the down section signal has been increased in height. *Both John Hunt*

No D259 enters a snowbound Levisham with the very last 08.55 Whitby-York train on 6 March 1965.

In the second picture a very run-down Levisham station is viewed from the famous 'Phoenix' railbus trip to Pickering High Mill on 20 July 1969, on what was billed as the last train to Pickering before track-lifting started from Summit.

Seen from a similar vantage point, it is a very different view from the DMU on 29 December 2017. *Maurice Burns/ Nick Carter/John Hunt*

The Borrows well tank No 3 and *Salmon* have attracted an admiring and, no doubt, curious crowd of onlookers during a stop for examination and replenishment of water supplies on 30 March 1969. Note the young plantation on the hillside. Hidden by the chimney, Maurice Burns carries out lubrication.

Fifty years later the coniferous trees have reached maturity and have recently been felled in this 9 April 2019 view, as No 26038 shunts at the station. The concrete gatepost and NER sign on the extreme left, and gate in the fence on the right, are common to both pictures. *John Boyes/John Hunt*

These two snowy views of Levisham signal box are dated 2 March 1965 and 28 November 2010. Little has changed except that the running-in board has been replaced, afforestation has covered the hillside beyond, and a replica weighbridge building has appeared, constructed behind the signal box in 2008.
Frank Dean/Simon Barraclough

A DMU waits in the platform as the 12.16 service to Malton on 2 March 1965.

Since then the up platform has been extended southwards and the sidings realigned in the 1970s in this view of No 101685 in the station on 18 February 2015. *Frank Dean/John Hunt*

A three-car Metro-Cammell DMU, on hire from BR, stands at Levisham forming the NYMR's first public train to Pickering (not to Malton – yet!) on 22 April 1973. On the right there used to be a siding, seen clearly in the previous 'past' picture.

On 17 October 2019 No 101685 awaits departure as the 12.30 Grosmont Pickering service. While the platform extension and new siding preclude an exact comparison, the outlines of the waiting room and signal box are common to both pictures. *David Idle/John Hunt*

No 61002 *Impala* sets off towards Pickering and its home depot at York on 2 March 1965.

During the First World War the line was singled between Levisham and New Bridge, just north of Pickering, the materials being utilised elsewhere to serve the war effort; the second track was never replaced. In the 'present' view, No 45212 is in the process of running round its Santa train on 7 December 2008. *Frank Dean/Philip Benham*

Pickering

The Gloucester C&W DMU is inspected at New Bridge after a test trip to the temporary platform at High Mill on 21 April 1974, before the inauguration of regular services from Grosmont the following day.

No 101685 accelerates away from New Bridge crossing forming a service to Grosmont on 25 March 2017. *Nick Carter/John Hunt*

No D2066 shunts in New Bridge quarry for the last time on the occasion of the final trip working of the pick-up goods between Malton and Pickering on 1 July 1966. In a similar view on 19 April 2019 there is no trace of the railway whatsoever. *Frank Dean/John Hunt*

No 5428 brings the BR weedkilling train past the temporary platform at High Mill on 6 May 1974. This was erected for the commencement of through services on 22 April of that year, but was removed following restoration of access into Pickering station just over a year later on 24 May 1975.

On 30 March 2017 No 46100 *Royal Scot* drifts in to Pickering, past the site of the temporary platform, with a train from Grosmont. *Both John Hunt*

Initially services beyond Goathland were operated by a three-car Metro-Cammell DMU hired in from BR because there was as yet no access to the station at Pickering, and there was no locomotive run-round facility at High Mill. Eventually negotiations to secure Pickering station were successful and trains began operating along the full length of the line from 24 May 1975. The first NYMR public train comprised the hired-in unit, which is seen in the first picture at High Mill on 22 April 1974. Two Gloucester DMUs are seen in the second view at High Mill on 31 March 1975.

On 4 April 2017 unit No 101685 passes the site. Note that the running line in the two earlier pictures is now a carriage siding, the old up line having been reinstated. *David Idle/ Chris Gammell/ John Hunt*

There was a 50-foot turntable at High Mill in 1893, but it was removed in 1958 and the pit filled with rubble from the demolished adjacent High Mill signal box in 1970. Here, Stephen Mason (left) and Dave Torbet are in conversation with Dave Fenney while clearing out the old turntable pit in the winter of 1996. The turntable itself, recovered from York Railway Museum (the former York North motive power depot) in 1993, is in the background. It was commissioned in 1998, and in the 'present' view No 62005 is turned by fireman Pete Maynard on the now extended 60-foot turntable on 26 April 2015. *Both John Hunt*

The BR weedkilling train, hauled by No 5428, arrives at Pickering on 6 May 1974. An exact 'present' comparison is difficult since the carriage works and associated sidings now occupy the land in the foreground of the 'past' picture, and tree growth has obscured the background, including the spire of the parish church. The 'Q6' awaits departure on 13 November 2018. *Both John Hunt*

No 5428 is seen again in Pickering with the BR weedkilling train on 6 May 1974. Pickering Castle dominates the skyline to the top right of the picture.

On 1 November 2014 No 44806 is in almost the same position while running round its train, which stands in platform 1. *Both John Hunt*

No D8568, still in Ribble Cement livery, stands in Pickering station some time in March 1987. The 'present' picture is from a similar viewpoint but this time with DMU No 101685 ready to depart with an early morning service to Grosmont on 11 February 2019. A lot has changed in the intervening period: the overall roof, to a G. T. Andrews design, was completed in 2011, the footbridge came from Walkergate on North Tyneside, following electrification of the Tyneside Metro, and was erected in 1996, and the single-storey building on the left came from Whitby Town and was erected in 1992/93. *Both John Hunt*

No 3442 *The Great Marquess* is seen during a stop at Pickering while on a filming run for the BBC on 13 April 1964. A cameraman attends to his equipment on the tender!

At the same location 53 years later, on 28 December 2017, the DMU is leaving for Grosmont. In the interim the platform has been lengthened, in 1991, and the carriage works just glimpsed on the right constructed in 1983. *David Mitchell/John Hunt*

During its stop on 13 April 1964, No 3442 receives the attention of photographers and the BBC cameraman on the tender.

On 28 March 1969, two industrial steam locomotives – Borrows 0-4-0WT No 3 and Andrew Barclay 0-6-0ST *Salmon* – arrived at Pickering and were steamed through to Grosmont two days later.

On 5 April 2017 No 44806 crosses the same bridge, No 7, over the Pickering Beck. *David Mitchell/ John Boyes/John Hunt*

The lone running-in board stands on the desolate and overgrown platform at Pickering in December 1970. The houses on the skyline remain the same in the 30 March 2017 view of platform 1, with part of the 'Whitby' building occupying the site of the forlorn running-in board shown in the earlier picture. *P. Walton/John Hunt*

No 5 brings a special fact-finding train for members of North Riding County Council into Pickering on 23 July 1971.

On 18 February 2018 No 926 *Repton* enters the station with the LNER teak train. The footbridge and tree growth hide the background, but the stone station wall on the extreme left is common to both pictures.
Both John Hunt

This is the Park Street exterior of Pickering station, pictured shortly before closure in March 1965. In the very similar view on 26 March 2017 not a lot has changed. *Frank Dean/John Hunt*

Standard tank No 80135, No 20 *Jennifer* and No 31 *Meteor* are stored in platform 1 on 20 April 1973.

At the Spring Steam Gala on 1 May 1998 No 34027 *Taw Valley*, carrying 'Golden Arrow' regalia, passes the replica *Rocket*.

In the third picture No 46100 *Royal Scot* enters the station on 29 March 2017.
David Idle/John Hunt (2)

In the first picture No 61319 leaves Pickering with a Whitby-York train in July 1964, in the second No 60886 eases out of the station with the empty Royal Train on 3 June 1965, and in the third No 45407 has run into the headshunt in order to run round its train on 5 April 2017.
Frank Dean (2)/John Hunt

It is the Royal reopening day of 1 May 1973, and Nos 29 and 2392, at the end of their historic journey, meet the crowds at Pickering.

No 46100 *Royal Scot* runs into the headshunt at Pickering to run round its train on 25 March 2017. The building above the cab, the former HSBC bank building, and the brick wall on the right are common to both pictures. *Geoff Plumb/John Hunt*

A welcoming throng has gathered at the junction of Park Street and the Market Place in Pickering as HRH the Duchess of Kent (in the light blue hat and coat, left of middle of the picture) mingles with the crowd following arrival of the reopening train on 1 May 1973. In the background can be seen Nos 2392 and 29.

Looking from the same vantage point on 19 April 2019, the buildings are largely unchanged, but while the crowds have gone the 'J27' features in both pictures. *Both John Hunt*

The 'past' view of Pickering station, looking north, dates from 1968, and was taken from the then still extant Bridge Street signal box.

The 'present' view was taken on 4 March 2019, but as the signal box was demolished in 1969/70, how to get a similar vantage point? An innovative solution was to take the picture from the top deck of an East Yorkshire Motor Services route 128 Scarborough-Helmsley service bus between its Ropery Lane and Middleton Road stops! Much has changed in the intervening period: while the building on the left (now NYMR offices) remains (with the salvaged Bridge Street signal box nameboard preserved on its street façade), the slate-roofed brick lean-to has gone, as has the loading dock, though a short length of track has been laid in its place to house a couple of wagons used for storage. The new overall roof now hides the castle, but the other buildings on the right, in Park Street, are easily recognisable. Instead of the level crossing gates, a stone wall now marks the southern limit of the NYMR. *Nigel Trotter/John Hunt*

Hauled by No 60886, the empty stock of the Royal Train eases over Bridge Street level crossing towards Hungate crossing, visible in the distance, on 3 June 1965. The same location is seen on 6 February 2019. *Frank Dean/John Hunt*

No 61021 *Reebok* shunts Pickering goods yard on 13 April 1964. The roof of the NER gas retort house can be glimpsed above the tender of the 'B1' and the wagons.

The old gas retort house is now a hairdressers and a road – The Ropery – together with the library on the right and a car park on the left, occupy the former railway land. In the layby stands an EYMS bus on service 128, which operates between Helmsley, Pickering and Scarborough and serves the same settlements as the Forge Valley line from Mill Lane Junction in Pickering to Seamer. Opened on 1 April 1882, it closed as early as 3 January 1950. More than 70 years ago, the precursor of the 128 bus could have been a 'G5' or even an NER Sentinel steam railcar! *David Mitchell/John Hunt*

The scene in the goods yard at Pickering on 28 March 1969 shows Andrew Barclay 0-6-0ST *Salmon* and Borrows 0-4-0WT No 3 arriving on their respective low-loaders. Following unloading, they were both steamed through to Grosmont on the 30th.

    Looking from the same viewpoint on 26 March 2017, The Ropery road now runs through the site of the goods yard and a car park covers the land once occupied by the goods shed and running lines.
Maurice Burns/John Hunt

Marishes Road station house and level crossing are pictured here in January 1965; the line would close to passenger trains two months later on 8 March.

In the same view on 16 October 2019, although the station house has lost one of its Andrews' chimneys it is in very good order as a private dwelling. Even the platforms remain, as well as the concrete lamp post and the down-side waiting shelter. *Frank Dean/John Hunt*

Rillington Junction station is seen here probably in the early 1950s, with the junction for Pickering and Whitby just visible beyond the far end of the down platform. The station is remarkably intact bearing in mind that passenger services were withdrawn from all intermediate stations between York and Scarborough (except Malton and Seamer) in the 1930s.

On 14 February 2019 a Class 185 DMU dashes through Rillington forming the 12.46 Scarborough-Liverpool Lime Street service. The station house remains, though considerably altered.
Ken Hoole, Frank Dean collection/John Hunt

Unit No 155342 heads the 05.00 Blackpool North-Scarborough service away from Malton on 13 March 2001. To the left of the train, in shadow, can be seen the southern abutment of the bridge that carried the Gilling-Driffield line, which also crossed the River Derwent to the right, where two of the bridge piers still stand.

No 185151 is also seen east of Malton forming the 08.56 Liverpool Lime Street-Scarborough service on 14 February 2019. The left-hand bridge abutment is still extant, as is the river bridge pier visible in the earlier picture, though now hidden by tree growth. *Both John Hunt*

No 5972 *Olton Hall* passes Malton signal box with the morning 'Scarborough Spa Express' from York on 19 August 2003.

One of the newly introduced five-car Nova 3 units, headed by No 68023 *Achilles*, passes the same location as the 08.54 Liverpool Lime Street-Scarborough service on 24 January 2020. *Both John Hunt*

No D2066 shunts the goods yard at Malton with the final pick-up goods from Pickering on 1 July 1966.
Seen from a similar vantage point on 14 February 2017, the stone-capped brick pillar at the end of the station platform, seen on the left in the 'past' picture, can just be discerned to the right of the first car on the left. *Frank Dean/John Hunt*

These two interesting views of Malton station were taken from the long since removed island platform on 14 May 1964. Hidden in the shadows in the first picture is the unique drawbridge that swung out from under the down platform to form an even walkway for passengers to the island platform, its operation being interlocked with the signalling. Also featured in the picture is Malton signal box; this, together with Malton West signal box, disappeared when the island platform was removed, the goods yards closed, track rationalised and the semaphores replaced by colour light signals in 1966. *Both John Boyes*

Malton locomotive depot is seen first on 5 April 1958 with 'J39' No 64928, 'G5' No 67248 and 'J27' No 65827 on shed, then on 20 March 1966 in the throes of demolition. Looking from the same vantage point on 14 February 2019, there are no clues that there was ever a locomotive shed here. *P. B. Booth/ John Boyes/John Hunt*

In October 1988 No 150206 stands in Malton station forming an evening Scarborough-Liverpool service
   On 17 October 2019 a new CAF Nova 3 train departs from Malton as the 12.56 Liverpool Lime Street-Scarborough service. Although the overall roof has gone and the part of the platform adjacent to the running line has been raised, the gable of the original station roof and the location cabinet on the right are common to both views. *John Spencer Gilks/John Hunt*

No 61018 *Gnu* shunts the 6.45am York-Whitby pick-up goods at the west end of Malton station on 14 May 1964

A similar view on 14 February 2019 features the unusual sight of Freightliner No 66951 passing en route to York. At that time, train crew manning the TransPennine Express Nova 5 test trains prior to their introduction in September 2019 were using the 66 for route learning. While the down line is in the same place, the station car park and housing occupy the land where *Gnu* was shunting. *John Boyes/John Hunt*

The first rolling stock to arrive on the fledgling preserved railway was AC Cars railbus No W79978, seen arriving at Grosmont on 9 August 1968, having travelled under its own power from Grangemouth in Scotland.
 In a similar location, No 155319 is leaving Grosmont in May 2002 having been used by Northern Rail for defensive driving training on the 1 in 49 gradient between Grosmont and Goathland. *John Boyes/John Hunt*

In the winter of 1931 platform 1 at Grosmont is cleared of snow by either Jack Elwick or Freddie Dickinson of the LNER's station staff. The picture is also interesting for showing the Hoffman kiln at the brickworks, built in 1923.

The second view along the Esk Valley platform was taken in June 1964.

Finally, moving forward to 17 June 2006, No 33025 heads the 'Whitby Jet' railtour returning to Carnforth. *NYMR collection/Frank Dean/ David Warren*

This is bridge 82 over the River Esk in Glaisdale gorge, with 'G5' No 67343 crossing at the head of a Stockton-Whitby train in August 1953.

In the 'present' picture the same vantage point is obscured by trees, but a Class 156 unit is crossing as a Middlesbrough-Whitby service on 3 April 2017.
J. W. Armstrong/ John Hunt

No 142015 emerges from the same girder bridge over the River Esk forming a Whitby-Middlesbrough service in March 1998.

No 66034 is at the same location with empty ballast hoppers returning from the NYMR to Tees Yard on 1 March 2017. *John Spencer Gilks/John Hunt*

No 62005 threads Glaisdale gorge with a winter special from Grosmont to Battersby in March 2005, then on 8 March 2017 No 66078 is seen negotiating the gorge with empty ballast hoppers, again returning from the NYMR to Tees Yard. *Both John Hunt*

Nos 63395 and 29, en route from Thornaby to Grosmont for a new life on the NYMR, run alongside the River Esk in Glaisdale gorge on 20 June 1970.

At the same location on 21 March 2010 No 30926 *Repton* heads a Whitby-Battersby service towards Glaisdale. *John Hunt/Ken Snowdon*

A Metro-Cammell DMU leads an Esk Valley service from Middlesbrough into Glaisdale in the winter of 1973.

No 156475 arrives at Glaisdale forming the 10.20 Middlesbrough-Whitby service on 3 April 2017. The typical LNER fencing remains, but the delightful lower-quadrant bracket signal, NE Region tangerine running-in board and lamp have all gone. *John Spencer Gilks/John Hunt*

'Past and present' at Glaisdale: the signal box is seen in 1994 and on 3 April 2017. *John Spencer Gilks/John Hunt*

An HST arrives at Glaisdale on 27 April 1991 with an excursion from London King's Cross to Whitby. The steep road up Limber Hill is clearly visible.

No 30926 *Repton*, with No D7628 on the rear, departs from Glaisdale with a 'Santa Special' to Battersby on 22 December 2009. *Both John Hunt*

Two Class 142 DMUs bound for Middlesbrough leave Glaisdale and cross a typical girder bridge over the River Esk in March 1994.

In a similar location, No 61264, with No D7628 on the rear, undertaking a crew training run from Grosmont to Battersby, has just crossed the rebuilt bridge on 4 February 2017. *John Spencer Gilks/John Hunt*

No 2005 is captured near Lealholm in the Esk Valley with a train from Whitby to Battersby on 8 June 1975. Forty-four years later not a lot has changed as No 76079 passes the same location with a service to Battersby on 26 June 2019. *John Whiteley/John Hunt*

No 2005 leads a two-car Gloucester C&W DMU, No D5032 and No 2392 towards Lealholm on 29 March 1982.

In the second picture, also approaching Lealholm, 'Royal' No 47798 heads the Royal Train conveying HRH The Prince of Wales from London Euston to Glaisdale on 14 May 1998. No 47799 is on the rear.

Finally, No 66078 heads for the NYMR with loaded ballast hoppers from Tees Yard on 8 March 2017. *All John Hunt*

At Park End, between Danby and Castleton, No 61264 heads the 'Esk Valley' railtour on 22 March 2014, running from York to Whitby via Darlington; the photo was taken on the return run from Whitby to Battersby with the 'B1' leading from Whitby and 'K4' No 61994 at the rear. The 'B1' returned to Grosmont from Battersby while the 'K4' took the train on to York.

No 70000 *Britannia* passes the same place with an NYMR Sunday dining train for Battersby on 12 May 2012.

Also at Park End, No 156490 forms a midday service from Whitby to Middlesbrough on 23 January 2017.
Ken Snowdon/Philip Benham/John Hunt

No 2005, with a textbook light grey exhaust, heads up the Esk Valley between Castleton and Commondale with a Whitby-Battersby excursion on 8 June 1975.

Class 156 unit, No 156479, passes the same location as the 11.58 Whitby-Newcastle service on 5 April 2019. *Peter Robinson/John Hunt*

Two Class 142 DMUs , forming a Middlesbrough-Whitby service, run between Kildale and Commondale in the summer of 1997.

On 20 March 2019 No 66114 heads a train of autoballasters destined for a track-relaying site south of Grosmont on the NYMR. *John Spencer Gilks/John Hunt*

With St Cuthbert's church prominent on the right, No 143014 departs from Kildale as a Middlesbrough-Whitby service in the summer of 2000.

No 156463 leaves Kildale forming the 10.20 Middlesbrough-Whitby service on 14 April 2018. The spire of the church is just visible through the trees. *John Spencer Gilks/John Hunt*

Viewed from Dundale Beck Farm, and with the backdrop of the Cleveland Hills, No D5500 tows No 63460 away from Battersby towards Kildale and Grosmont on 7 April 1978.

A Class 156 DMU in seen in almost the same location forming the 14.02 Middlesbrough-Whitby service on 5 April 2019. *Both John Hunt*

No 2005 climbs away from Battersby with a return excursion from there to Whitby on 15 June 1975.

On 5 April 2019 unit No 156479 passes the same location as the 10.20 Middlesbrough-Whitby service.

Finally, Colas No 56094 climbs away from Battersby towards Kildale with the train of auto-ballasters from Doncaster bound initially for Whitby, depicted on page 149. The tree on the left has grown considerably in 45 years, as have the lineside bushes, but the outline of the Cleveland Hills is still unmistakeable
All John Hunt

Battersby to Middlesbrough

Nos 31413 and 31417 tail 'The Esk Valley Fellsman' charter train from Whitby to Carlisle away from Battersby towards Middlesbrough on 16 May 1993.

At the same location No 66114 approaches Battersby with auto-ballasters from York to Grosmont (NYMR) on 21 March 2019. Visible to the right, on top of Easby Moor, stands Captain Cook's Monument.
John Spencer Gilks/John Hunt

The 07.20 Middlesbrough-Scarborough DMU approaches Battersby on 4 May 1963.
    The young tree in the 'past' picture now obscures the view, but on 1 December 2016 No 156490 approaches the junction with a morning service from Middlesbrough to Whitby. *John Boyes/John Hunt*

No 37419 takes the Middlesbrough line at Battersby Junction with 'The Esk Valley Fellsman' from Whitby to Carlisle on 16 May 1993.

No 57316 brings up the rear of a Whitby-bound charter on 7 April 2017. 10½ is the mileage from Guisborough Junction at Middlesbrough. *John Spencer Gilks/John Hunt*

No 142065 leads another Class 142 unit into Battersby from Middlesbrough in March 1994.

No 156480 arrives at Battersby as the 10.20 Middlesbrough-Whitby service on 15 February 2019.

In the same location, Colas No 70807, with No 56094 on the rear, arrives at Battersby in dire weather with a train of auto-ballasters from Doncaster, bound initially for Whitby, then an engineer's possession at Danby, on 22 February 2020. In recent years infrastructure trains have been hauled by Class 66 diesels and the appearance of Class 70 and 56 diesels was only a fairly recent occurrence. *John Spencer Gilks/ John Hunt (2)*

With the Cleveland Hills as a backdrop, No 69866, with a train from Middlesbrough to Whitby via Picton, has just finished taking water at Battersby on 16 August 1954.

In the second picture two three-car DMUs, full of day-trippers returning from the seaside at Whitby, leave Battersby for Middlesbrough on a balmy summer's evening in 1964.

Although the semaphore signal has gone, more than 50 years since the end of regular steam operation the water column still stands as No 156482 prepares to leave Battersby on 7 April 2017.
J. W. Armstrong/ John Boyes/John Hunt

Nos D6899, 63395 and NCB 29 arrive at Battersby on 25 June 1970 en route from Thornaby to Grosmont.

DMUs forming services to and from Whitby stand in Battersby station as No D5500, hauling 'Q7' 0-8-0 No 63460, bound for the NYMR, waits to follow the Whitby train on 7 April 1978.

Having changed ends, the driver of No 156480, forming the 10.20 from Middlesbrough, is changing single-line tokens on the platform before resuming the journey to Whitby on 15 February 2019.
All John Hunt

The 18.00 DMU from Middlesbrough to Whitby arrives at Battersby on 29 April 1963.

No 5690 *Leander* has attracted a large – for Battersby! – crowd of onlookers following its arrival on a balmy summer's day in July 1983 en route to the North Yorkshire Moors Railway. Note that in the period between the two pictures the lamps have been replaced, the run-round loop on the left has been lifted and the vegetation has grown up; otherwise very little has changed. *John Boyes/John Hunt*

A DMU working the 17.37 Middlesbrough-Guisborough service passes Morton Grange gate box on 25 April 1963. In the distance stands the unmistakeable outline of Roseberry Topping, at a height of 1,056 feet.

A Class 142, forming the 11.41 Newcastle-Danby, passes Morton Grange on 11 March 2019, a crisp spring day that highlights Roseberry Topping. The crossing cottage is hidden by coniferous trees and a new bungalow has been built on the right. *John Boyes/John Hunt*

A DMU calls at Great Ayton with a Middlesbrough-Whitby service on 25 May 1965. The line up to the coal drops is still in situ and, though devoid of wagons, the yard is still in use for coal distribution.

No 156439 arrives at Great Ayton forming the 12.41 Newcastle-Whitby service on 22 February 2020. Rationalisation has meant the disappearance of the station building, seats and running-in board. The coal drops are derelict and the yard overgrown, though the house gable on the left is common to both pictures. *John Spencer Gilks/John Hunt*

No D5500 leads No 63460 towards Morton Grange on 7 April 1978. Beyond the trees the line swings sharply to the right at the site of Nunthorpe East Junction and heads for Battersby.

At the same location on 11 March 2019 a new industrial development has appeared on the left and the crossing cottage is obscured by trees as No 156469 passes Morton Grange as the 11.58 Whitby-Newcastle service, although the outline of Guisborough Moor remains the same. *Both John Hunt*

Following an overhaul at ICI Wilton, No 2005 makes its way back to Grosmont and runs into Nunthorpe station in April 1986, then in the 'present' view No 142066 arrives at Nunthorpe as the 10.41 service from Newcastle. *Both John Hunt*

Two locomotives from the National Collection, Nos D5500 and 63460, are seen at North Ormesby en route from the NRM at York to the NYMR on 7 April 1978.

No 156472 passes the same spot as the 10.20 Middlesbrough-Whitby service on 29 March 2019. Part of the transporter bridge, now painted a striking blue colour, is still visible but the track has been singled and the whole backdrop has been hidden by tree growth. *Both John Hunt*

With Middlesbrough's iconic transporter bridge over the River Tees as an imposing backdrop, No 2238 leads No 2392 (not in steam) and No 2005 past Guisborough Junction, Middlesbrough, heading up the bank to Nunthorpe at North Ormesby on 22 December 1975. The locomotives had been in Thornaby roundhouse since appearing at the S&D 150 celebrations at Shildon in August of that year, and were on their way back to the NYMR.

An exactly identical viewpoint is not possible as the signal from which the 'past' picture was taken has long since gone and the inevitable tree growth hides the view, but this vantage point, some yards further south, shows No 185126 shunting onto the Whitby branch before returning to Middlesbrough station on 11 March 2019. Part of the transporter bridge is visible and the lines to Redcar and Saltburn run on the other side of the fence above the 185, but the docks, ships and cranes are just a distant memory. *Both John Hunt*

No 67754 stands in the bay platform at the east end of Middlesbrough station with a service to Whitby and Scarborough via the coast. It is 3 May 1958, the last day of services via the coast line. After No 67754 has departed, No 69877 will place its train into the platform before taking a Whitby service via Battersby.

   The edge of the platform in the 'past' picture is just visible, though very overgrown, and two of the buildings above the two steam locomotives are still extant as No 66099 passes with a Scunthorpe-Lackenby steel train on 29 March 2019. *R. F. Payne/John Hunt*

Postscript: a dedication

This and previous volumes have relied heavily on the sources of original 'past' pictures, and these have predominantly come from the collections of the Armstrong Trust, David Sutcliffe, David Mitchell, John Boyes, Michael Mensing, John Spencer Gilks and last, but by no means least, Frank Dean.

While the contributions of the aforementioned are very much appreciated, as the pictures have formed the essential foundation of each of the books, the pictures of the late Frank Dean should be singled out.

Frank Dean, railwayman, historian, film-maker and a supporter of the NYMR since its inception, passed away on 24 November 2018, aged 93. One of his duties as a railwayman was to prepare the plans and documents for the BR Signal & Telegraph Department inspection trains, and this enabled him to travel over much of the North Eastern Region. He also joined the Chief Civil Engineer's inspection specials when an S&T representative was needed. Frank made good use of the opportunity to take photographs, an activity that received his supervisors' unofficial support. They also turned a blind eye to his occasional driving turns on the York 'B1' that normally powered the specials.

Frank and his parents had been frequent travellers on the lines to Whitby, so when he heard that they were threatened with closure, he asked for special permission to film the last days of service. The result was *A Sentimental Journey* and *On the Whitby Branch*. His wife, Heather, accompanied him while filming, sometimes driving the car when they were 'chasing' a train, and also taking a keen interest in the finished products, which appeared under the general label 'Country Films'. Many of the films have been selected for the Yorkshire Film Archive and will be available for future generations to enjoy.

Frank Dean in impish mood during his 90th birthday celebrations at Grosmont. *Maurice Burns*

The NORTH YORKSHIRE MOORS RAILWAY people

Any railway, let alone a heritage one, can only operate with people. The NYMR has successfully existed with a combination of paid staff and volunteers virtually since its inception in 1967. The former are increasingly essential in a business that, in 2019, had a turnover of more than £5.1 million, carried 320,000 passengers and employed more than 100 paid staff, augmented by seasonal staff in critical areas such as catering. However, the Railway cannot operate without a tremendous input of volunteer labour. For example, locomotives are almost exclusively crewed by volunteers, especially trained and assessed so that they can also operate over Network Rail lines to Whitby and Battersby. All other departments have crucial volunteer input

too, but Station Groups, dedicated to each station on the line, and other supporting organisations such as the LNER Carriage Association and the North Eastern Locomotive Preservation Group, are entirely volunteer run, and make a valuable contribution to the success of the Railway. Crucial, too, are the Junior Volunteers, so important for the future of the Railway. Special events, visits of celebrities, filming, and awards and rewards are also an important part of NYMR life.

The pictures that follow show the staff and volunteers who help to make it all possible, at work – and play! The pictures on this and subsequent pages therefore illustrate some of the many and varied people, tasks and activities that contribute towards the successful operation of the Railway.

NYMR Junior Volunteers have graduated to became firemen on the NYMR as well as on the main line, such as Phil Akester seen here firing the iconic *Flying Scotsman*.

Motive Power Department

Junior Volunteers clean 'B1' 4-6-0 No 1264 at Grosmont MPD on 18 August 2018 in readiness for a visit from a film crew.
Roger Swift

MPD fitter Owain Samuel poses with the newly overhauled valve crosshead, die blocks and pin for BR Standard 2-6-4T 80136 on 20 December 2019.
NYMR

The NYMR employs apprentices, and here are two in the Motive Power Department, Finn Allen (left) and James Woodland, on 27 October 2019. *NYMR*

Steam engines are dirty work! MPD fitter Phil Naylor (left) and fireman John Kirk take time off for a chat at Grosmont shed on 8 September 2019. *Andrew Jeffrey*

While steam is the mainstay, and what the NYMR's customers want to see, diesels play an important role in keeping the Railway's trains running. Here Nick Simpson, Bob Fussey and Josh Smith are seen with a diesel engine crankshaft on 18 May 2017. *NYMR*

The overhaul of 'Black Five' 4-6-0 No 44806 started at Grosmont on 29 February 2020 and the young team involved pose for the camera. On the loco are Phil Akester, Luke Taylor, Rob Morgan, Eoin Cuddy and Andrew Jeffery. On the ground are Thomas Dibbs, Barney Casey (in the pit), Adam Holmes, Richard Turton and Tom Houseman. *Andrew Jeffery*

Charlie Dore gives the thumbs up on the overhaul of '9F' 2-10-0 92134 on 24 September 2019. *Andrew Jeffrey*

Driver Neal Woods and fireman Phil Akester are with 'Q6' 0-8-0, as LNER No 2235, ready for *Downton Abbey* filming at Pickering on 12 November 2018. *John Hunt*

Driver Neal Woods is seen again with fireman Alexandra Jolly on 'K1' 2-6-0 No 62005 on 2 September 2018. *John Hunt*

Driver Matt Fisher and Sarah Pennington, one of the regular New Bridge engine cleaners, are on 'B1' 4-6-0 No 1264 on 21 October 2019. It's a family affair, as her sister Kathryn is also a cleaner, and their dad Mark is a fireman. *D. Pollard*

The NYMR's Peter James (left) and Chris Cubitt with Irish Rail trainees Keith Farrelly and Connie O'Gara (right) at Grosmont on 10 October 2017. The NYMR has been used to train Irish footplatemen on steam so that they can operate the steam locomotives of the RPSI on its regular steam excursions in Northern Ireland and in the Republic. *John Hunt*

With its background of running regular services over the Network Rail line between Whitby, Grosmont and Battersby, the NYMR provided expertise and training to the North Norfolk Railway towards its aim of running over the NR line between Sheringham and Cromer. Here NNR and NYMR crews pose in front of BR Standard 2-6-0 No 76084 at Cromer on the first training run on 6 June 2017. *NYMR*

Carriage & Wagon Department

Jonny Haw works on the windows of Mark 1 coach TSO 5000, while in the foreground are a pair of bogies overhauled at the NYMR's Kirby Misperton workshop, which were having the finishing touches applied by Richard de Sadeleer on 29 February 2020 ready to be fitted under Mark 1 TSO 4290. *John Hunt*

Dave Jakeman works on the replacement of crash pillars on the end of one of the Railway's Mark 1 coaches on 2 January 2008. *John Hunt*

Mark Toyne finishes Pullman car *Garnet* in the C&W paint shop *NYMR*

Peter Whittaker carefully and expertly signwrites Gresley buffet car No 641. *NYMR*

East Coast Joint Stock coach No 189 and volunteers were photographed in the Atkins restoration shed at Pickering on 1 September 2018. From the far end, they include David Young, Marcus Woodcock, Russ Whitwam, Gordon Wells, Paul Johnson, Dave Cullingworth, John Sutcliffe and Chris Johnson. Standing on the far left is Mike Faulkner, with Nick Stringer on the right. *Murray Brown*

NYMR Wagon Group volunteers are at work on brake vans in the C&W workshop at Pickering on 3 June 2017. On the brake van veranda is Mike Faulkner, on the scaffolding tower is Malcolm Broadhead, and in the background Neil Young. *Ian Broadhead*

Permanent Way Department

Infrastructure work takes place in all weathers and at any time of the day or night. Here, in rather hostile conditions, S&T staff Ray Halmshaw, Mike Holmes and Peter Emerson are drilling holes through the rails for rebonding the track circuits near Trout Farm after track relaying at Pickering on 30 March 2018.
Craig Donald

Right: If work on or around the track is necessary when trains are running through the day, there is often no alternative but to work through the night. Here Peter Smeaton loads overburden into the dumper truck at midnight in the remote depths of Newtondale on 28 August 2017.
Simon Barraclough

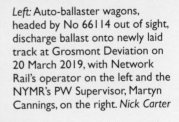

Left: Auto-ballaster wagons, headed by No 66114 out of sight, discharge ballast onto newly laid track at Grosmont Deviation on 20 March 2019, with Network Rail's operator on the left and the NYMR's PW Supervisor, Martyn Cannings, on the right. *Nick Carter*

Levisham Station Group volunteers Stephen Mason, Michael Miller and Simon Barraclough are assisting the PW Department by clipping new rails to concrete sleepers in Northdale on 14 January 2017. *Simon Barraclough*

Eric Barraclough, Bob Boyt, Phillip Buckle, Michael Miller, Andy Napier (hiding) and Martin Robinson change sleepers at Levisham station on 19 March 2018. *Simon Barraclough*

John Liddel explains to volunteers, including John Mallam, John Merrick, William Nutbrown, James Conway and Gary Stainburn, what the tamper does at New Bridge on 3 February 2019. *Bryan Blundell*

Martyn Cannings (left) and Peter Smeaton sit in the cab of tamper No 73250, with Nick Carter and Bryan Blundell visible in the ballast regulator in front, returning to New Bridge from tamping at Fen Bog on 9 November 2018. *Ed Holman*

Dave Osborne fixes the 'prize length' sign to its new base at Goathland. Such signs denoted lengths of award-winning permanent way in LNER and BR days. *Mike Braham*

Peter Emerson and, on the right, Ray Halmshaw work on a point motor in the rain south of Levisham loop on 19 March 2019. *Craig Donald*

Signal & Telegraph Department

In rather better weather conditions, S&T staff and volunteers are laying cable troughing at Trout Farm between New Bridge and Pickering, as No 62005 passes with a train from Grosmont on 31 December 2019. *Simon Barraclough*

Using the PW crane, one of the 'dolls' is lifted into place on the signal gantry immediately north of Grosmont station on 29 December 2013. The gantry, refurbished and shortened, was formerly located at Falsgrave, Scarborough. *Craig Donald*

Signalman and Goathland Station Master John Bruce is photographed at work, but on a busman's holiday at Bridgnorth on the Severn Valley Railway on 3 August 2018. *Maurice Burns*

Lineside

The clearance of unwanted lineside vegetation is an ongoing process: here Levisham Station Group volunteers Michael Miller, Stephen Mason and Phillip Buckle clear and burn lineside scrub near Platelayers Cottages, north of Levisham, on 9 December 2017.
Simon Barraclough

A Sunday Squad of Junior Volunteers poses in front of their dry-stone walling handiwork at Beckhole on 15 April 2018.
Roger Swift

A record turn-out of fencing team volunteers pose after completing recent work in Northdale on 17 June 2019. Left to right, they are Gary Moss, Phil Atkin, Adam Hurford-Smith, Geoff Preston, Cath Moss, John Hardcastle, Ian Johnson, Bill Alexander, Adrian Nelson and Terry Sellars. *Richard Simpson*
   No 5428 passes the Levisham Station Group fencing team of Lee Buckle, Michael Miller, Phillip Buckle and Stephen Mason at MP13, north of Levisham, on 12 May 2019. *Simon Barraclough*

Major projects

Despite the inclement weather conditions that plagued the project, Construction Marine, VolkerRail and NYMR staff and volunteers celebrate the lifting into place of the new bridge No 30 on 11 February 2010.
John Hunt

Pete Waterman is interviewed for the TV cameras at the formal commissioning of the new bridge on 19 April 2010.
John Hunt

Goathland looks neat and tidy in this view taken in August 1961. The signal box appears to be switched out. Note the BR camping coach in the up sidings. In the foreground is bridge No 27. *David Sutcliffe*

The same view is seen on 8 May 2020 following replacement of the main span and reinstatement of the up and down running lines. Following inspection in 2018, bridge No 27 over the Eller Beck at Goathland was deemed life-expired and required urgent replacement. Thanks to financial support from the NYMR's Yorkshire's Magnificent Journey appeal, with major funding from the Heritage Lottery Fund, it was renewed early in 2020. This picture was taken after the railway should have reopened to passenger trains, but the final alignment, levelling and tamping of the track, the reinstatement of S&T equipment and the subsequent running of trains were put on hold on because of the Coronavirus pandemic that year. Having just crossed the new bridge, No 08556 and brake van are on their regular weekly line inspection from Pickering New Bridge to Grosmont and back. *John Hunt*

The Grosmont Station Group team pose by the finished job of painting Station House on 7 May 2018; they are Paul Cawthorne, Brian Cawthorne, Victor Wood and John Guy. *Peter Robinson*

Keeping the NYMR stations spick and span is a never-ending job. Here, Station Group volunteers Jon McGott, John Guy, Brian Carter and Paul Cawthorne paint the Grosmont ticket office building on 20 May 2019. *Peter Robinson.*

Caution
Cleaning
Charging

Pickering Station Group volunteers apply white lining to the edging of platform 2 on 21 February 2018. Nearest the camera is Andrew Frith, with Geoff Smith, John Lamey and Michael Cook beyond him. *Peter Carleton*

For the second year running, the Tour de Yorkshire passed through Grosmont, this time on 4 May 2019. Crowds lined the street and steam engines were lined up, whistles blowing: 'B1' No 1264 is on the right and No 80136 out of sight to the left. *Andrew Jeffrey*

A velocipede event took place between Pickering New Bridge and Levisham on 9 November 2019. Here participants, with several of the various velocipedes, await the 'right away' at Levisham. *John Midcalf*

Levisham, with its spacious and ideal paddock, accommodates marquees for special events such as the annual '60s Weekend'. Here, appreciative crowds listen to 'Elvis' on 14 July 2018. *Simon Barraclough*

Catering staff in action, including Caron Webster, Patience Hibbert, Katherine Watson, Robin Fosker, Duncan Longworth and Maureen Skelton, photographed in the catering marquee during 'Wartime Weekend' at Levisham on 12 October 2019. *Simon Barraclough*

In a busy scene at a gala beer festival at Goathland, there are no fewer than 16 hand pumps in use! Behind the bar are Michelle Osborne, Margaret Braham, David Hardwick and Dave Osborne. *Mike Braham*

For many years the NYMR has held a 'Wartime Weekend' in October, which brings together a host of re-enactors, such as those in these two scenes. The first was recorded in one of the Railway's superb LNER coaches, while the other is in the waiting shelter at Goathland.
Both John Hunt

Yorkshire Volunteer Corps of Drums march off platform 2 at Grosmont on the Sunday of 'Wartime Weekend' in October 2019. *Peter Robinson*

The Knightingales perform their 1940s repertoire at Levisham during 'Wartime Weekend'. *John Hunt*

'Santa Specials' are a vey popular feature of the NYMR's season. Here Margaret and Gary Stainburn, festively attired, keep Santa company on 1 December 2018. *John Hunt*

At one of the Railway's traditional Christmas get-togethers, on 19 December 2004, MPD staff Bob Bullock, Rob Russell, John Hunt and Phil Naylor relive the 1950s. *John Hunt*

No 63395, transformed as No 2235 for its starring role in *Downton Abbey*, waits in Pickering – or supposedly King's Cross? - station for the next call from the film crew on 13 November 2018. *John Hunt*

NYMR staff assisting in the filming were, left to right, Kieran Murray, Darren Palmer, Dave Tibbet, Matt Donald and Stuart Bell, seen on the same day against a backdrop of 'J27' No 65894. *Terry Newman*

At the south end of Pickering station, the former signal box from nearby Marishes Road has been re-erected as a demonstration box. Here two young visitors are shown the ropes by one of the station staff on 28 May 2015. *NYMR*

The NYMR has a branch of the RMT Union. Here Paul Whickham, Steve Elliot, Caroline Stewart, Dave Tibbet, Tammy Naylor and Ray Stewart wait with their traditional banner to join the parade in the Durham Miners' Gala on 16 September 2016. *Courtesy of a passer by!*

Levisham's Artist in Residence, Chris Ware, sketches 'Q6' No 63395 on 13 September 2007. *John Hunt*
    Visiting TV celebrities Sara Cox and Rufus Hound chat to driver Chris Cubitt during filming at Grosmont on 15 November 2011. The Railway hosted part of their Lottery Good Causes week-long camper-van tour of the UK, with Sara riding on No 76079 to Pickering. *John Hunt*

On 13 April 2019 the Permanent Way Department's paid staff, volunteers and partners' annual outing took place in the GWR inspection saloon, affording an opportunity to socialise with the departmental chief, Nigel Trotter (second from left). *Nick Carter*

On 22 August 2019 the Railway recognised and rewarded those volunteers who had given 50 years service to the NYMR. Here they pose for the camera with their certificates. Front row, left to right, are John Hunt, Ray Sowerby, Terry Newman, and Chris Cubitt. Back row, left to right, are Chris Lawson, Nigel Trotter, Neil McDonald, Nick Carter, David Torbet and Ian Varty. *NYMR*

At the 2018 Heritage Railway Association Awards, held in London on 6 December, the NYMR won the London Underground Operational Enhancement Award for the restoration of Goathland station, waiting room and shop. Left to right are John Bennett and John Bruce (Goathland Station Group), Edmund Bird, Heritage Advisor to Transport for London, and Mark Carne (former Network Rail CEO) at the presentation of the award. *HRA*

At the annual HRA Awards ceremony held in Birmingham on 8 February 2020, Matthew, Heather and Howard Self (the owners) and Charlie Dore (MPD) collect the *Steam Railway* Award for the restoration of 9F 2-10-0 No 92134 from Nick Brodrick (right) on behalf of the magazine's readers. *HRA*

List of Subscribers

Steve Alder

Ian James Allison

Emma Anderson

Keith Archer

Robert Armstrong

Pete Ashford

David Aspinall

Trevor Baker

Ian Beckerson

Chris Beicher

John Blackburn

John Bodicoat

Stephen Bonnington

Peter & Clare Bowes

Neil Brook

John Bryan

David Burgess

Kevin Bygrave

Robin Cain

John Carr

Steven Carter

Andrew R Cattell

Geoffrey Catterick

Perry Stephen Cliff

List of Subscribers

Mike Close

Ian Cook

Graeme Cook

Jon Cousens

Ian Crane

Stephen Crane

Arthur Crofton

A N Danks

Stuart K Dark

Trefor Davies

Michael Denholm

Chris Dickinson

Les Dobson

MW Dodd

John Doubleday

Sidney Dowson

Dave Dukes

Jamie Dunn

John Edmundson

John England

Danny Fawcett

Robin Fisher

List of Subscribers

Barry Fletcher

Christopher Forder

John Freear

John Garde

Stewart Garvey

Michael Gibbon

Chris Grayson

Brian Green

James Gurnett

Martine Gwynne

Peter Hall

Graham Halliday

John Hammond

John Hawthornthwaite

Derek Hemmingway

Peter Hempson

Keith Herlock

Colin Hilburn

Peter Hill

Keith Hills

Christine Hodgson

Adam Holmes

List of Subscribers

Frank Horsfield

Norman Hugill

Harold Hull

Angela Hunt

Andy Hutchings

James Isherwood

Paul Jameson

James Jefferies

Douglas Kipling

Carlton Lagusz

Fred Landery

C Lawson

Roger Lazenby

Christopher Lindley

Simon Long

Steve Long

Alastair Lunn

Maurice Miles

List of Subscribers

Ian Millership

Don Murray

Jim Neal

Phillip Newton

Stephen Nuttall

Pippa Page

Robert Parkin

Mike Parkin

Andrew Paton

John Pearse

Keith Porter

Richard Postill

Stephen Rhodes

Phil Robinson

Stan Robinson

Anthony Rosier

List of Subscribers

John Rutherford	Jens Strain
Tina Saunders	G Strange
Paul Scrimshaw	Stuart Talton
Peter Sheasby	Adrian Thomas
Derek Shorten	Jeff Thomas
Michael Simms	Karl Thompson
Michael Smith	Alan Walker
Les Smith	Bob Watson
John Spalding	David Webb
Luke Stirzaker	Paul Welton

List of Subscribers

Mark White

Richard Whiteley

Michael Willcock

Mark Withers

Ian Wood

Charles Wright

Pauline Wright

Derek Young

Publisher's Dedication

The 'footplate crew' at Past & Present Publishing would like to place on record their appreciation of the enthusiasm and support that has been so much in evidence from The North Yorkshire Moors Railway throughout the preparation of this volume.

The restoration of the line is another inspirational example and represents and reflects the true spirit and ongoing hard work, dedication and determination of all those who are working to rebuild and develop Britain's Heritage Railways.

Glossary

AB	Andrew Barclay	NER	North Eastern Railway
BBC	British Broadcasting Corporation	NR	Network Rail
BR	British Railways	NY&CR	North Yorkshire & Cleveland Railway
C&W	Carriage & Wagon	NYMHRT	North Yorkshire Moors Historical Railway Trust
CL	Composite lavatory coach		
DMU	Diesel multiple unit	NYMRPS	North Yorkshire Moors Railway Preservation Society
GNR	Great Northern Railway		
GWR	Great Western Railway	PW	Permanent way
EWS	English Welsh & Scottish Railways	RAF	Royal Air Force
K&ESR	Kent & East Sussex Railway	RCTS	Railway Correspondence & Travel Society
LMS	London, Midland & Scottish Railway	RSH	Robert Stephenson & Hawthorn
LNER	London & North Eastern Railway	S&T	Signal & Telegraph
LNERCA	LNER Coach Association	SLS	Stephenson Locomotive Society
M&DR	Malton & Driffield Railway	ST	Saddle tank
MPD	Motive power department	W&PR	Whitby & Pickering Railway
NCB	National Coal Board	WT	Well tank
NELPG	North Eastern Locomotive Preservation Group	Y&NMR	York and North Midland Railway
		YN&BR	York, Newcastle & Berwick Railway

Index of locations and locomotive classes

Locations
Battersby 145-152
Beckhole 51, 177
Darnholm 55
Fen Bogs 77-81
Glaisdale 134-137;
  gorge 130-133
Goathland 3, 56-70, 174,
  176, 180, 184, 185, 192;
Summit signal box 75-76
Great Ayton 154
Grosmont 33-50, 128-129,
  167, 171, 176, 181, 186,
  190;
  carriage & wagon 168-170;
  loco shed 45-48, 163,
  164;
  Tunnel Cottages 44
Kildale 142-144
Larpool Viaduct 17-22
Lealholm 138-139
Levisham 89-97, 172, 174,
  177, 178, 183, 184, 186, 190
Malton 120-127
Marishes Road 119, 189
Moorgates 71-74
Morton Grange 153, 155
Newtondale 85-88, 171
Northdale 82-84, 172, 178
Park End 140-141
Pickering 98-118, 165, 173,
  175, 182, 188, 189
R100
Ruswarp 25-28;
  Chain Bridge Cottages 28
Sleights 29-31
Water Ark 52-52
Whitby 7-16;
  Prospect Hill Junction 18-
  19

Steam locomotive classes
'5600' 0-6-2T 39
'A4' 4-6-2 53
'A6' 4-6-2T 78
'A8' 4-6-2T 150, 159
'B1' 4-6-0 9, 14, 27, 32, 55,
  58, 59, 78, 80, 96, 112, 117,
  127, 132, 137, 140, 166
'Battle of Britain' 4-6-2 52
'Black Five' 4-6-0 11, 16, 20,
  21, 51, 55, 64, 68, 80, 96,
  100, 103, 104, 112, 164, 178
'BR 4MT 2-6-0 138, 167, 190
'BR 4MT 2-6-4T 58, 83, 111,
  162, 167, 182
'BR 9F 2-10-0 165
'Britannia' 4-6-2 140
'G5' 0-4-4T 125, 130
'Hall' 4-60 122
'J27' 0-6-0 3, 43, 74, 113, 114,
  125, 158, 188
'J39' 0-6-0 125
'J52' 0-6-0T 39, 67, 90
'Jubilee' 4-6-0 152
'K1' 2-6-0 12, 13, 15, 16, 21,
  22, 23, 26, 34, 41, 91, 102,
  138, 139, 141, 145, 156,
  158, 166, 175
'K4' 2-6-0 106, 107
'L1' 2-6-4T 159
Mirvale 0-4-0ST 63, 64, 79, 87
No 3 0-4-0WT 40, 54, 93,
  107, 118
No 5 0-6-2T 66, 73, 77, 81,
  82, 109
No 20 0-6-0T 111
No 29 0-6-2T 48, 63, 72, 74,
  113, 114, 133, 151

No 31 0-6-0T 111
'P3' 0-6-0 50, 68, 74
'Q6' 0-8-0 41, 45, 53, 66, 68,
  70, 75, 84, 90, 103, 133, 151,
  158, 165, 188, 190
'Q7' 0-8-0 144, 151, 155, 157
Rocket 111
'Royal Scot' 4-6-0 82, 100,
  111, 113
'S15' 4-6-0 51, 73
Salmon 0-6-0T 40, 64, 93,
  107, 118
'Schools' 4-4-0 34, 109, 133,
  136
'V2' 2-6-2 112, 116
'WD' 2-10-0 34
'West Country' 4-6-2 38,
  54, 111

Diesel locomotive classes
03 99, 123
08 180
17 105
25 63, 69, 71, 137
26 93
31 29, 144, 146, 151, 155, 157
33 129
35 'Hymek' 38, 79
37 15, 35, 148, 151
40 92
47 69, 139
56 145
57 148
66 50, 70, 71, 127, 131, 132,
  139, 142, 146, 159
70 149

DMU classes
142 10, 131, 137, 142, 149,
  156
143 143
144 23
150 126
155 121, 128
156 7, 8, 10, 12, 26, 29, 30, 31,
  35, 134, 140, 141, 143, 144,
  145, 147, 149, 150, 151, 154,
  155, 157
185 120, 121, 158
220 52
AC railbus 62, 66, 71, 128
'Heritage' 7, 8, 11, 13, 17, 19,
  21, 24, 36, 40, 55, 56, 61, 67,
  72, 75, 79, 81, 91, 92, 95, 96,
  98, 101, 105, 106, 134, 147,
  150, 152, 153, 154
HST 136
Nova 3 122, 126

Captions for pages i-vii

Page i
No 825 crosses the River Esk at Ruswarp on 29 October 2008. *John Hunt*

Page ii
No 4771 *Green Arrow* leaves Levisham with the LNER teak train on 14 March 2003. *John Hunt*

Page iii
No 6023 *King Edward II* and No 6990 *Witherslack Hall* sandwich No 62005 outside Deviation shed at Grosmont on 25 September 2019. *Paul Jameson*

Page iv
No 60019 *Bittern* at Thomasson Foss between Grosmont and Goathland on 4 April 2008. *John Hunt*

Page v
No 60163 *Tornado* passes the motive power depot with the 09.30 from Grosmont to Pickering on 8 May 2009. *Robin Patrick*

Page vi
No 63395 pilots No 65894 at Green End on NELPG gala day 26 September 2019. *Ken Snowdon*

Page vii
No 80136 deep in the heart of Newtondale with the 11.00 Pickering to Grosmont service on 26 April 2019. *Ken Snowdon*